The Practitioner's Guide to **RPA**

The Practitioner's Guide to **RPA**

A practical guide for deploying
Robotics Process Automation

Jonathan Sireci

Copyright 2020 Farchair Solutions, LLC.

All Rights Reserved. Printed in the United States of America. No part of this publication may be reproduced, stored in or introduced into a digital archive, or transmitted, in any form, or by any means (electronic, mechanical, photocopying, recording or otherwise), without the prior permission of the publisher. Requests for permission should be directed to contact@farchair.com with the subject "Permissions Request".

ISBN: 9798606434510

CONTENTS

	Preface	i
1	Introduction	1
2	What is RPA?	4
3	What is the Difference Between AI and RPA?	7
4	Is RPA Right for My Company?	23
5	Where Should I Start?	28
6	Identifying RPA Opportunities	32
7	Selecting a Vendor	44
8	Building Your Business Case	66
9	Deploying RPA	71
10	Small Businesses and RPA	79
11	Historical and Ethical Considerations	81
12	Conclusion	91
	About the Author	93

FIGURES

3.1	Business Automation Ecosystem	8
3.2	RPA Architecture	13
4.1	RPA Fit in Context of Business Capabilities	24
4.2	RPA Value to Effort By Business Unit	26
5.1	End to End Process Framework	30
6.1	Happy Path Volume Mapping	38
7.1	RPA Vendor Fit Grid	54
7.2	RPA Cost Models	57
7.3	Bot Per Process vs. Bot Per VM	60
11.1	Industrial Revolution Grid	83

PREFACE

There is a large gap in business literature between academic and consulting frameworks on one side and step by step "how-to" guides on the other. Scholarly works often result in overarching summaries of business dynamics that provide executives with the big picture but do little to help turn the principles into reality. Consulting literature is more detailed but there is an inherent tension between a consulting firm's desire to openly share information and their existential need to sell knowledge about how to operationalize the strategies they recommend. On the other extreme, there hosts of "how-to" books that explain with varying levels of relevance the detailed tactics of behind important business topics. The irony that plagues many of these sources is that the more detailed they are, the more brittle they are. Brittle in the sense that the detailed information does not always age well nor can it be broadly applied to the spectrum of situations represented by the readers.

Is it possible to create a durable, concise and operationally relevant resource for important business topics? I believe so and this is the goal of "The Practitioner's Guide to RPA". The insights provided in this book are likely different than others you've read and there are good reasons for this. First, it's written from the perspective of someone who had to learn about RPA and deploy it without the aid of large consulting firms. There was no help coming and we had to find ways to figure RPA out on our own. Second, the conclusions are not prescriptive in the sense of a how-to manual. Instead, the recommended steps should be viewed as a practical narrative from which you may glean insights that can help you navigate your own situation. Last but not least, the perspective of this guide blurs the line between the strategic and the tactical. Practitioners have to straddle this line every day and you will likely feel the tension. In the end, it is my hope that you find this brief guide thought-provoking, helpful and relevant.

1

INTRODUCTION

My first exposure to RPA was in 2015 while working as a Shared Services Strategy Consultant. At the time, our 3-year plan was full of huge Accounts Payable (AP) opportunities with ROIs too large to ignore. The problem was that these investments required huge capex and opex investments on the front end in order to achieve the target ROI within 3 to 5 years. We needed buildings with capacity to hold between one and three thousand employees, amenities, communications infrastructure, office furniture, computers, software and in-house-developed tools just to get the doors open.

As you can imagine, the search for alternatives began before the budget was even finalized. The risk that the shared services center would not be able to meet ROI was high given the fact that the difference between success and failure hinged on our ability to train highly complex procedures executed manually in a green-screen program to new staff indefinitely. What could go wrong? Our leadership also recognized that 3 to 5 years is an eternity for shareholders conditioned to expect fast shared services ROI because of the numerous outsourcing alternatives to our insourced shared services model.

Two main alternatives emerged as the budget for the manual approach was approved. First, we could outsource the whole operation. It would be someone else's problem and we could impose an ROI demand on the partnership. Second, we could explore automation opportunities created by emerging technologies. A member of our enabling technologies team had been researching the potential use cases for a growing technology called Robotics Process Automation or RPA. One of our top IT resources and I were asked to investigate the feasibility of these tools to help create the efficiencies required to reduce the projected staffing demand for around three thousand FTE.

Ultimately, RPA helped the organization avoid having to staff between 1,000 and 2,000 FTE while generating verifiable ROI that made our leadership think our internal rate of return (IRR) values were completely made up (not many leaders have seen an IRR in the thousands before). While RPA was instrumental in achieving this goal, the process was not perfect or for the faint of heart. We got out of RPA what we put into it and there were many lessons learned.

I always believed a book would be a more

consumable and lasting way to communicate the principles of RPA. From defining what RPA actually is versus how a vendor will explain it to you, to how you select the right tools and which opportunities you should pursue, this book is meant to share insights from a practitioner's perspective that may help you make better strategic decisions.

2

WHAT IS RPA?

Robotics Process Automation or RPA is a complicated name for a tool that, in practice, is very simple. RPA tools provide a way for an individual with limited coding ability to configure an automated workflow leveraging the user interface for applications that they routinely use on their desktop. Think Excel or Access macros on steroids. A full RPA tool will also provide a way to schedule, load balance and scale process automations. If this "simple" explanation sounds confusing, don't worry. Keep reading and these terms will make more sense in context.

One of the biggest barriers to understanding RPA is the whole idea of "robotics". If you are like me the first thing that comes to mind when I hear the word "robotics" is something metal with a bunch of wires buzzing around a car manufacturing plant welding pieces of steel together. I think of a Rumba, Battlebots or any number of machines with a remote control that you can touch, feel or crash into something. To understand "robotics" in an RPA context you have to put the physical references aside and consider the more accurate term "software robotics". Another name for "software robotics" is simply "bots".

"Bot" may sound more familiar to many of you and it is likely that you've heard it used in negative contexts. If you've heard of a Directed Denial of Service (DDoS) attack on a website, these attacks are marshalled using "bots" or machines that are being controlled centrally and running a common script telling them to access a website over and over again. This context is the genesis of "robotics" in the name RPA – a central controller directing scalable software resources to perform a common process. It's also the reason I believe there are so many RPA startups with connections back to government cyber defense organizations. I am not surprised anymore when I meet new RPA vendors that have leaders in the company with a CIA or defense industry connection.

As you can imagine, it would be a harder sell for vendors if they called RPA "Bot Process Automation" given the negative connotations of "bots". The people who build RPA tools use the more formal, sophisticated term "robotics" instead to sidestep these negative connotations. While the term

"RPA" is an accurate, succinct explanation of what these tools do and how they work, the term is confusing to the same demographic that RPA vendors are trying to sell the tools to – people with limited technical skills but deep business process knowledge.

The terminology around RPA becomes even more hazy when vendors try to sell RPA tools as Artificial Intelligence (AI) tools. AI and RPA are very different. AI leverages data to create insights that can be used to create better processes. RPA creates and runs specific, clearly defined processes. While the two can be paired, thus creating "intelligent automation" solutions, RPA vendors tacking the AI label on their tool is technically inaccurate.

3

WHAT IS THE DIFFERENCE BETWEEN AI AND RPA?

Many RPA vendors indiscriminately mix "AI" terminology into their sales pitch so it's important to get a handle on the difference between the two. RPA and AI differ in architecture, focus and outputs but that does not mean they can't work together. RPA and AI are major components in the business automation ecosystem that includes scripting tools, process automation tools and artificial intelligence tools. Intelligent automation joins process automation tools, like RPA, with AI tools. Before diving into the differences between RPA and AI, let's set the stage by explaining the business automation ecosystem.

Business Automation Ecosystem

Let's assume that the business automation ecosystem represents the full set of automation tools required by all organizations. This will by definition exclude systems that automate core, industry specific niches and instead highlight the tools that are common across industries. Each tool plays a role in driving greater transactional efficiencies over time and each tool has unique limitations.

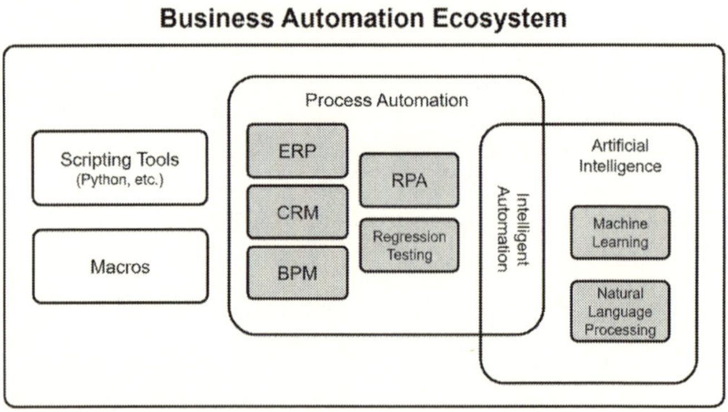

Business Automation Ecosystem

Figure 3.1 Business Automation Ecosystem

Macros and Scripting Tools

The use of macro-based and script-based automations is common across all organizations and functions. They fill perceived automation gaps left by rejected enterprise level automation priorities. If IT can't get a needed automation built into other core systems or the request is a low priority on an infinitely expanding backlog, leaders may look to fill these gaps with macros and scripting tools.

Consider the fact that most organizations depend on macros run through Microsoft Office products to automate a large number of transactional tasks. If you have not encountered this yourself, start asking around, especially in your back-office teams. I guarantee you will find the exercise eye-opening.

There are huge advantages to having the ability to build macros that fulfil de-prioritized enterprise automation requests. First, you are able to save FTE for the automated tasks. Second, there is usually no cost except the time you allow someone on your team to build and maintain the scripts. Third, IT has very little interest in monitoring the use and development of macros. The time to govern versus the benefits gained do not add up so business areas that rely on macros tend to value the autonomy these tools enable. Last, it shifts the focus of the team to more strategic parts of their workflow.

The benefits may sound great but what are the downsides? First, these scripts are usually invisible to IT. Many of you may be thinking, "That's not a downside." While this may be true in the short and middle term, IT can't support what it can't see. Maintaining macros is not difficult while the author still works for you but the minute that person leaves, it is very difficult to keep them in working order, troubleshoot the occasional error or make updates. Second, macros absorb the value that could have justified investment in a permanent solution. If you create real value with a macro, why should finance agree to invest in a tool that will solve the problem more sustainably? I've seen finance reject these business cases before essentially trapping the business area in its own ingenuity. Last but not least, macros cannot interface with all of the applications you likely need to automate a workflow from start to finish. Macros can interact in a limited way with non-Microsoft programs, however only the smallest automation opportunities can be fully automated using macros.

Scripting tools, like Python, are more powerful than macros but still suffer from the same disadvantages. Unlike macros, Python can interface with web-applications through free extensions like Selenium generally providing better ability to automate a process end-to-end. While powerful, scheduling and maintaining Python scripts outside of a tightly managed development framework can open up unintended security vulnerabilities. Many organizations regulate the use of Python to prevent the potential security ramifications.

While macros and scripting tools can produce automation outcomes quickly and affordably, they can result in unintended consequences for businesses over the long term. As you will learn, RPA can provide a more robust alternative for macro and scripting options while mitigating many of the negative consequences.

Process Automation Tools

Process automation tools help businesses build structured workflows for common and essential tasks. Examples include core Enterprise Resource Planning (ERP) systems, Customer Relationship Management (CRM) tools, Business Process Management (BPM) software, regression testing tools and RPA. ERP systems act as a workflow engine and system of record for key HR, Finance, Payroll and Supply Chain tasks. CRM tools enable workflow automation for case and knowledge management across multiple customer contexts. Business Process Management tools offer a generic workflow engine that can fill in the process gaps left by other core systems. BPM systems often blur the lines between ERP and CRM tools. Regression testing tools help automate routine testing for system changes and upgrades. Last but not least, RPA helps tie together disparate systems and data into unified, cross-application workflows.

Process automation tools share three key features that set them apart from other tool sets. First, their core purpose is to automate linear workflows. Second, these systems provide foundational reporting from the data generated through these workflows. Third, process automation tools often act as systems of record for employee, financial, customer support and sales funnel information. More and more process automation systems are integrating aspects of machine learning and natural language processing into their platforms, however, AI simply enhances how individuals access workflows and data. Driving linear, transactional workflows is still the core function of process automation tools.

While some will argue against characterizing RPA as a process automation tool, the reality is that RPA at it's core is nothing more than a nimble workflow engine. It does not act as a system of record for key business data like other process automation tools but when you cut through the AI-hype, RPA has much more in common with process automation tools than machine learning or natural language processing applications. In fact, RPA tools and regression testing tools are almost identical in the way that they are set up and leveraged yet I have yet to find a regression testing system vendor claim that their tools are "AI". There are significant differences between AI and RPA so to better understand the differences between them, let's start by breaking down RPA.

RPA Architecture

There are 4 main components that underpin RPA solutions:
1. RPA Application
2. Virtual Servers and Virtual Machines
3. Database
4. RPA Controller

RPA Architecture

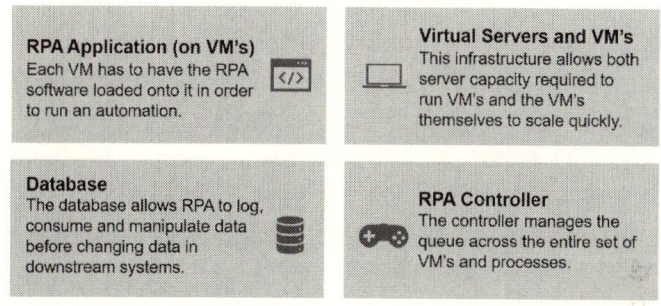

Figure 3.2 RPA Architecture

RPA Application

The RPA application is the part that you'll usually see in a vendor demo. All RPA applications have a way to document processes, a way to run those processes and a way to debug processes. The UI for RPA process documentation methods vary from using a drag-and-drop library of functions into a vertical list of the business process steps to creating Visio-like diagrams with properties tied to the shapes. Some RPA tools can record actions performed by the process designer. The part of the RPA application you can't see is that each application creates a scalable unit, meaning each machine you load the application onto can be centrally controlled. While the RPA application is the most visually appealing aspect of an RPA tool, it is not the most valuable feature of an RPA solution.

Virtual Machines and Virtual Servers

The RPA application is loaded on virtual machines or distinct desktop-like environments that reside on a server rather than a personal computer. A virtual machine is loaded with the same applications that a person would use along with the RPA application. Virtual machines become your scalable work unit meaning as demand for a particular RPA process increases, the more virtual machines you can leverage against the demand, the faster that volume can be worked.

Virtual machines exist on servers or virtual servers. Either can work but in my experience, decoupling your virtual machines from a physical server and instead deploying the virtual machines on a scalable cloud infrastructure is more cost effective and more responsive to changes in demand. As your requirement for virtual machines increases, your demand for cloud computing resources will increase as well. Ensure that you leverage infrastructure that will balance the need to be responsive to variability in your process demand with the need to be cost effective.

Database

The database component of RPA solutions does exactly what you think it does and maybe a little bit more. The database logs the activities of each VM including which process that VM ran, when it ran, whether the transaction was successful or not and time stamps every step along the way. Technically, the database is not doing any of this. All it does is record the activities passed to it by the controller and RPA application. But think about the power of this kind of data to further understand the process that you've automated. Being able to say with absolute certainty how many transactions passed and failed along with a log recording each step along the way is worth its weight in gold, especially in environments where there is high pressure to sustain year over year productivity improvements.

RPA Controller

The RPA controller is the most valuable part of an RPA solution. RPA controllers determine which processes each VM works on, automatically kicks off scheduled processes, load balance demand on the fly if VMs assigned to a specific process are maxed out, prioritize VM assignments real time, activate dormant VMs when volume spikes occur and surface executive and operational reports by process from the database. Without the controller, all you have is a scripting tool that has to be manually maintained by someone with superior technical abilities, usually the person who created the script. Without the controller, whatever automation script you create will not be easily scheduled, scalable or auditable. Try getting the same person who creates an automation script to build step by step logging into their code. You will watch the light fade from their eyes as they consider other employment opportunities. The RPA controller does the work no one, not even your most talented programmers want to do. As such, it is the component that should be most scrutinized during vendor evaluations.

What Problems Is RPA Built To Solve?

The book answer is that RPA is ideally suited to handle stable (I dispute this later), transactional, rules-based processes with structured digital data. The reason for this is that RPA will do exactly what you tell it to do. It does not think, it executes. If it runs into something unexpected or an error, it will stop running the script, log the error and move on to the next transaction. You are not buying a tool that will outline your processes for you. Instead, you are buying a tool that can help you more quickly automate processes you have more or less already defined.

Take a minute to think about the types of processes that meet all of the criteria listed above. It should not take you very long to realize that RPA is better suited to solve problems in some functional areas better than others. Finance processes, for example tend to more readily meet ideal RPA candidate criteria than Human Resources. Take the monthly financial close process for example. The inputs rarely change, the output rarely changes and the steps, while numerous also rarely change. There are isolated steps throughout the end to end process that may require human judgement but for the most part, finance processes are ideal candidates for RPA.

Human resources on the other hand is not as

straightforward. How do you define a process that will accurately handle every type of benefits inquiry that is received over the course of a month? Even if you could get individuals to fill out a form to structure the inputs for RPA, the number of output variations are tremendous and as complex as a human being's personal life circumstances. Is the task impossible? No. But are these the kinds of problems you want to tackle as a proof of concept? No.

RPA makes setting up automations easier, but it also allows you to go after automation ideas that may have been financially out of reach in the past. Some RPA vendors call these overlooked opportunities the "long tail of automation." The big automation opportunities are often tied to enterprise projects (ERP deployments, etc.) which drain the organization of the resources and cash that might otherwise be used to go after some of these smaller opportunities. The irony is that these "smaller" opportunities can represent huge cost savings when considered in aggregate. Prior to RPA, the business case to go after these smaller opportunities did not exist. Put simply, RPA allows you to automate well-defined processes that would have otherwise been dismissed or overlooked when compared to other opportunities.

What Is The Output of RPA?

The output of RPA is the completion of a previously manual transaction. Think about how many people in your organization complete repetitive transactions day in and day out. Let's say that you are on an HR sourcing team. Your overall job is to find the right candidates to apply to your organization's open positions. One of the best ways to cast a wide net with your job posting is to re-post it on external job boards. In order to do this, you have to copy all of the job posting data, login to the external job board, copy all of the data into the appropriate fields then submit the form. The ultimate output of the process is a job posting replicated on all of the relevant, external job boards.

At this point you've expanded the reach of a single job post but there are two problems. First, your job post still should be posted on a dozen more external job boards, so your work is just beginning. The process outlined above needs to be repeated for each external job board you are posting to. Furthermore, in order to prevent re-work or accidentally re-posting the same job again, you'll need to track which sites you posted the job to for each requisition you manage. The second problem is you are managing 20 to 50 job postings at any given time.

Do you see the issue? This process is inherently transactional, manual, time-consuming, costly to scale, repetitive, tedious, difficult for an individual to manually track and even more difficult for a manager to audit or measure effectiveness. Often times, sourcers will not have enough time to re-post their jobs to all of the relevant job boards so important avenues for attracting candidates are inconsistently leveraged or entirely neglected. This process is ripe for automation.

In this situation, leveraging RPA will optimize the desired outcomes expected from the manual process all along. In a perfect situation the sourcer would always post each job to the relevant external job-boards, track which sites they re-posted the job to, never accidentally re-post a job they already posted on that external job board, complete this task shortly after posting to the main job board and ensure that the external postings are taken down when the original job posting is filled. RPA can create all of these outcomes if the business process is well defined. In short, the outcomes created by RPA are the same outcomes expected of a highly proficient person doing the process manually.

How Is AI Different Than RPA?

RPA is not AI and AI is not RPA. RPA is a powerful process automation mechanism that mimics the way people perform transactional work on their desktop. AI is a generic term for many types of statistical automation methods that leverage machine learning (or the now vogue "deep learning") to process unstructured data sets and identify patterns within those data sets that would likely be unrecognized by manual efforts. What does this mean?

To understand what AI actually is requires a basic understanding of machine learning. Machine learning, at its most basic level, evolved as a way for databases to self-optimize based on usage patterns. If everyone is searching for candy bar sales data but the database has chip sales data indexed (prioritized) first, the search for candy bar sales will be slower. Machine learning allows the database to recognize how it is being used and re-index on the fly in order to improve access to the most relevant, high-demand data.

AI builds on the concept of statistical optimization by layering in other complex frameworks like natural language processing. Amazon's Alexa or Apple's Siri are a few ubiquitous examples of machine learning blended with natural language processing to create a complex simulation of human intelligence. When you talk to Alexa, a natural language processing algorithm analyzes the words that you used and the way that you used the words to categorize both the content of what you said and the context around what you said. This helps the AI make a more accurate interpretation of how to kick off a very targeted, accurate search for the information you are requesting. In short, AI combines machine learning (statistical automation) with other software capabilities to mimic human intelligence in a number of different ways.

Given the significant differences between AI and RPA, be confident when challenging vendors on their claims equating the two technologies. Many times, the AI component of what they are trying to sell is aspirational or in development. They likely want to use RPA to collect deep process data, centralize that data and run it through some complex statistical algorithms to create insights into your processes. This could leave an unaware or uninitiated company vulnerable to data hostage. Don't be fooled by vaporware. Proof of concept everything.

Why Are Corporations Investing In RPA?

Corporations are investing in RPA technologies because of the low up-front and ongoing investment costs and the enormous savings generated. RPA solutions are cheap when compared to the alternatives for many large corporations. Let's take the example mentioned earlier where we need to automate the re-posting of jobs on external job boards. What are the other technical alternatives a large enterprise might consider? A large company could try to develop an in-house application, seek out a very specialized vendor or create integrations from core systems to the external job posting sites. Developing an in-house application for something like this will result in a large resource commitment for the build, test, release and maintenance of the tool. Contracting with a specialized vendor will likely require an integration and will probably have a strange billing model that is out of sync with the value it actually produces. Building integrations with each site and your core system could be extremely time consuming if any of the sites actually allow you to build a direct feed into their systems. Not to mention the fact that a project like this will never stack up against other major enterprise initiatives. RPA sits in that financial sweet spot where the marginal costs are much lower than the marginal value. It does not require hyper-specialized resources to develop workflows, costly or exotic infrastructure to run and it does not take a long time to deploy.

RPA goes beyond cost avoidance by significantly reducing or eliminating the amount of time people spend "swivel chairing" between desktop applications trying to accomplish a single task. There are a myriad of situations that individuals are asked to do this kind of work. In many cases human beings are filling the roll of an extremely complex integration between systems that don't play well together. RPA is well suited for these use cases.

Another reason corporations are throwing resources at RPA is that RPA can transform the delivery of transactional work overnight. If your business already has a large team of specialists performing transactional work, RPA can eliminate the need for a large percentage of that work. If you are on the ball enough to build an RPA solution before you build out a large team of data entry specialists, you can avoid the opportunity costs associated with that team from day one. Remember that RPA success, like any other corporate investment, is not the result of tech-enthusiasm or disingenuous altruism. RPA solves problems in a very specific strategic niche and ROI is always expected.

4

IS RPA RIGHT FOR MY COMPANY?

RPA is a powerful tool but how do you know that it's a good fit for your business? Regardless of what consultants or vendors may tell you, the reality is that specific business contexts need RPA more than others. The following questions can help you determine how urgently you need RPA.

Does your IT department have difficulty building integrations quickly and accurately?

Some IT organizations are better equipped than others to build integrations between systems. Whether it's an issue of resource constraints or resource capabilities, some organizations are simply incapable of meeting all of the requested integration demands. On the other hand, organizations that can quickly respond to the need to build integrations between systems will have a less urgent need for RPA.

The reason for this is that RPA acts as duct-tape for situations where data needs to be shared between systems but an integration does not exist. Moving data from one system to another is something that RPA is good at but if you can build an integration one time to do the same task permanently without incurring additional future costs, integrations are usually the better option. However, if the backlog of requests for integrations is extremely long or your IT team does not have the ability to consistently deliver high-quality integrations, RPA may be a great solution for this business dynamic.

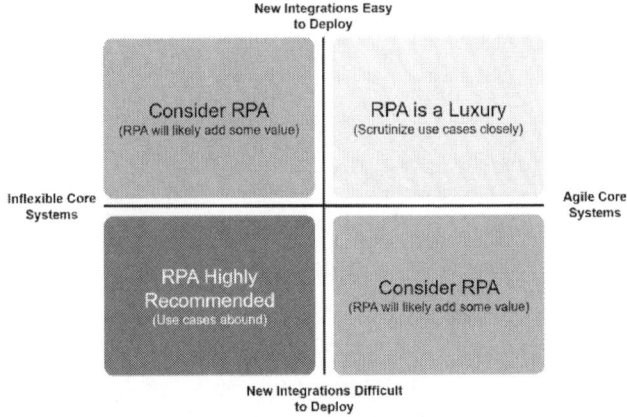

Figure 4.1 RPA Fit in Context of Business Capabilities

Are your core systems of record innovative and

flexible?

Organizations that have invested in innovative or flexible ERP solutions may not need RPA as urgently as other businesses. For example, if your ERP system has powerful three-way-match functionality that significantly reduces the time required to analyze differences between purchase orders, invoices and receipts, the potential value RPA can add is greatly diminished. Consider RPA a work-around for core systems that do not natively create the outcomes your business needs.

However, just because your core systems can theoretically create the desired outcomes, you cannot assume that those systems are flexible enough to quickly respond to your business need. Not all ERPs are equal in their ability to respond to business requirements in a nimble way. SAP for example is notoriously rigid in the way its databases are structured. Workday on the other hand has a high degree of flexibility in the way data can be leveraged within native business processes.

The moral of the story is that not all ERP systems or other core business systems are equal. Some are more rigid and hard to configure than others. If your core systems are agile, RPA may not be an urgent need. If they are brittle and difficult to configure, RPA may help you deliver outcomes more quickly.

Which functional areas have the most use cases?

All business units do not produce the same

value for effort with RPA. Finance and logistics are two examples where the value for effort is high whereas marketing and HR do not have high value for effort. While there may be a lot of RPA use cases in other business units, if there is a high degree of automation already present within the finance and supply chain areas, you may not produce the anticipated value from your RPA investment. This dynamic alone is not a reason to dismiss what RPA can do for your organization but it is a factor that should be analyzed before investing money and resources.

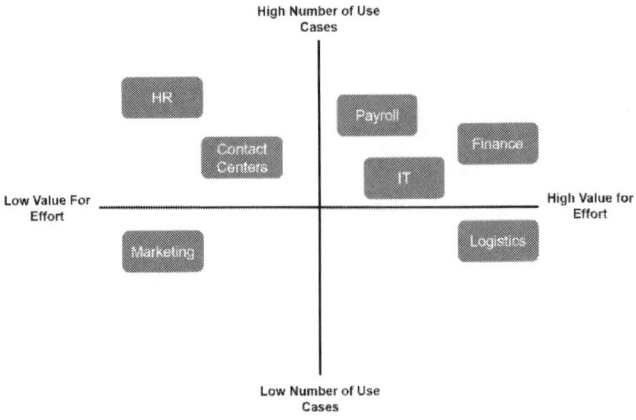

Figure 4.2 RPA Value to Effort By Business Unit

Does your organization need automation for cross-functional activities that can't be consolidated within core systems?

There are some business scenarios that cut across functional areas and are difficult to automate with traditional tools. One example of this is merger and acquisition (M&A) scenarios. M&A's require multiple business units to coordinate the analysis and synthesis of core business data and refinement of cross-functional business processes. RPA can be useful in M&A situations even if there is a high degree of automation within each business unit already. Consider whether these situations arise frequently enough in your organization to justify investing in a tool like RPA.

The bottom-line is don't be caught in a situation where you believe you have to deploy RPA to keep pace with competition. RPA is a tool like any other and the business context where you intend to deploy these tools is a key driver to determining where RPA fits in helping your organization achieve its goals.

5

WHERE SHOULD I START?

The best place to start to get RPA off the ground is to build clear business process documentation. Beyond just being good business practice, creating visibility into the way work is being performed in your organization will help you identify RPA candidates quickly and deploy RPA solutions faster. Another advantage to understanding your business opportunities thoroughly is the ability to identify a target proof of concept prior to submitting a request for proposals to RPA vendors. This may seem backwards, but it will save you money in two ways. First, identifying RPA opportunities and a potential proof of concept candidate prevents a vendor from trying to charge you consulting fees to do this work for you. Vendors love to work with organizations who have not done their homework on their own business processes.

"We can help you with that," will likely cost you anywhere from $50,000 to $120,000. This is the easiest money they will ever make. Second, identifying an RPA proof of concept before bringing in vendors creates leverage when negotiating with your finalists. Being able to give two finalist vendors the same process to prove the value of their tools gives you deep insight into how these tools actually work day-to-day and gives you leverage when you begin negotiating prices.

While process documentation may not seem like a difficult task to undertake, there are right and wrong ways to do it especially if automation is the ultimate goal. The best way to document processes for automation is to identify end to end processes then break out the key activities two levels down from the end to end process definitions. Level two and three process activities are usually where automation opportunities are identified in a top down approach. Many organizations have a patchwork of business process documents that vary in their level of detail, organization and traceability back to industry standard end to end process taxonomies. What does all that mean and why does it matter?

30 | The Practitioner's Guide to RPA

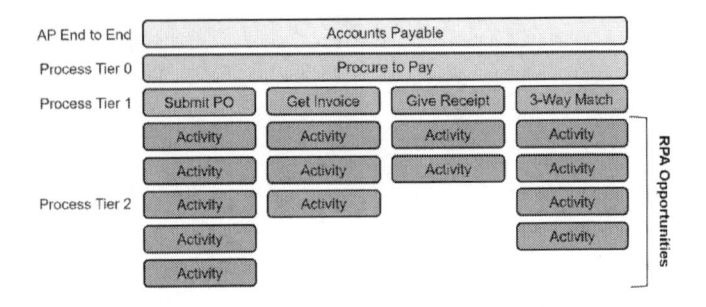

Figure 5.1 End to End Process Framework

Let's say you are trying to understand where you may have automation opportunities in an accounts payable environment. The end to end process might be called "Procure to Pay" while the level two might break that down that level 1 process into activities like "Submit Purchase Orders", "Receive Invoice", "Produce Receipt", and "Perform 3-Way Match". In this case, any one of these level 2 activities could be full of automation activities. Going a level deeper might expose specific parts of the activities that are more easily automated then others but zeroing in on what activities are good opportunities for automation is the first step.

The end to end process context within which those activities live allows you to determine the correct order to implement automation initiatives. In practical terms, it doesn't make sense to jump to solving a 3-way matching problem with automation if there is a known issue with the purchase order process. Solving the upstream activities first prevents you from inadvertently creating automated work arounds for the downstream impacts of upstream problems. Automation initiatives should be prioritized by upstream activities first and potential savings second. While this may seem counterintuitive, often the downstream inefficiencies that seem big (and appear to have large ROI) are being created by relatively small upstream inefficiencies. The only way to prioritize automation initiatives this way is to have an end to end framework in place to contextualize those initiatives.

What's the point of all of this effort on the front end? The answer is that you can save thousands if not hundreds of thousands of dollars in consulting fees if you conduct a survey of your own activities and create an RPA roadmap yourself. A consultant will be happy to accelerate some aspects of this process for you, but you'll eventually need to do this work anyway if you want to sustain your RPA function. If you have the time and resources to build your end to end framework and identify RPA opportunities before moving on to the next steps (selecting a vendor, etc.) you should. But what is the criteria for finding an ideal RPA opportunity?

6

IDENTIFYING RPA OPPORTUNITIES

The best way to identify RPA opportunities will depend on your circumstances. If time is of the essence, try to find anyone who is building macros or is copying and pasting data from one system to another. People who build macros are often manipulating data that core systems are not in order to accomplish a specific task. These data manipulations may help you zero in on low hanging fruit that comes with the added bonus of an invested, knowledgeable subject matter expert to help design the RPA process. The other place to look is for individuals who spend time copying and pasting data from one system to another as part of their process.

These tasks should be well suited for RPA automation.

Basic Selection Criteria

If you have time to be more methodical in your approach a good place to start is free literature provided by consulting organizations like Deloitte, EY, PWC, KPMG or Hackett. These companies publish very similar lists of general areas where RPA could be employed. These lists document broad areas of opportunity by functional area and in some cases by industry. This will help take you from a 30,000-foot view of where to look for RPA opportunities to a 10,000-foot view. The specific activities that can be automated within functional areas (Accounts Payable – three-way matching EDI exceptions for example) are not usually defined in these lists. To get to that next level you have to get into the details of your business processes.

The basic criteria for an ideal RPA use case are that the process is transactional in nature, the logic required to complete the transaction is rules based and the data required to run the automation in a structured, digital format. Transactional work has consistent volume and is repetitive. Every purchase order, invoice and receipt need to be matched even if the core auto-matching algorithm fails to create a match. This is an activity that must be done, has a consistent volume and is repetitive. A repetitive process is usually also a rules-based process. The idea of a process being rules based is that human judgement is not necessary to move the process forward. While a human being may be performing the process today, they are applying a set of consistent rules and criteria to the process that can be automated. In order to automate a set of steps that a person may be performing today, the data they are using to make decisions through the process must be available in a structured, digital format. RPA tools cannot consume pictures or images on its own without being integrated with an optical character recognition (OCR) system. RPA tools can usually consume a structured (non-picture) pdf file but the format and data arrangement needs to be consistent.

Beyond the basic criteria, there are three other criteria that should be considered: In-flight Initiatives, Achieving ROI and Process Stability. It is important to evaluate whether there are initiatives in flight that would permanently fix the problem you are trying to solve with RPA. For example, if you find a process where people are performing dual-data-entry tasks (moving data from one system to another through a user interface) and you discover that your IT department is building an integration to solve this problem, it may not be worth your time or resources to use RPA to solve this problem. An integration should permanently fix this issue whereas RPA would be a workaround. Another example is if a process involves extracting data from your ERP system, manipulating that data outside of the system then re-entering back into the system, you may be able to configure the workflow to account for this logic directly in the ERP system. If you can change the workflow within the ERP system, RPA is just a workaround, not a permanent fix.

Achieving ROI is the most important aspect of evaluating which initiatives to go after with RPA. If the cost to implement and maintain the process exceed the value you anticipate creating from that investment, you should not be pursing that particular process. This evaluation varies significantly depending on the cost model you have with your vendor (more on this later). For now, remember that while an RPA tool can help you go after smaller automation opportunities, the infrastructure and maintenance costs are not free so there will always be ideas that fall below the line.

Addressing Unstable Processes

Process stability is one of the most commonly recommended criteria to evaluate potential RPA candidates. The traditional argument is that the process should not be in a state of flux or redesign if you are going to leverage RPA to automate it. While this is ideal and makes the development of the automation easier, it should be considered a nice-to-have.

There are several reasons why you should not eliminate an RPA candidate because of instability but the most important one is that calling a process "unstable" doesn't really mean anything. What I mean is the term "unstable" is a generic label for complexity and reflects how frustrated individuals who manage the process are with the complexity. Labeling a process "unstable" does not help you understand why the process is unstable. Believe it or not, RPA tools can help you stabilize some of the root causes of instability. I prefer to label these types of processes as "apparently complex" because that term invites exploration and a better understanding of the underlying causes.

Apparently complex processes are very difficult to build standard operating procedures or training documents for and the outputs are difficult to validate. Some of the main characteristics that make a process apparently complex are incomplete data, multiple research branches, multiple resolution branches and multiple failure modes.

A process with incomplete data forces the person performing the process to make some sort of extrapolation about what to do next using the data they have. Extrapolating your way to a solution in these situations is really the process of identifying the right research and resolution steps for that particular problem. For example, if you have great purchase order and invoice data but your receipts are inconsistent or unreliable, an EDI matching algorithm will likely fail leaving a person to make a judgement call about how to reconcile the failed match. Many would look at a process like this and say that it's unsuitable for automation. The problem with that assumption is that the people performing the work are constantly making judgement calls and creating rules on the fly to impose order on the problem. In other words, the team manually performing the work is creating multiple ways of researching and resolving the same root problems.

The advantage of having a team manually resolve

apparently complex processes is that the business has unintentionally created a laboratory to discover the ideal method of overcoming the sources of process instability. Everyone performing the process is using slightly varying methods to overcome imperfect information and, in some cases, using different methods to resolve the same process branch. The disadvantage of this approach is the inconsistent outcomes created by team members' varying methods even for the same branch of a process. A manager of teams performing this work may struggle to report on the seemingly random outcomes being generated by their team. The root cause stems from having multiple ways to resolve the same branch of the process which will create a cascade of failure modes in the final outputs. Ultimately, "instability" or "apparent complexity" is the result of incomplete data that leads to extrapolation of research steps and resolution steps which, if performed inconsistently create a flood of failure modes.

So, what do you do with these types of processes? The most important fact to acknowledge first is that your laboratory is not filled with people who are equally proficient at making the right judgement calls. You have some rock stars who are better suited than others to make accurate extrapolations about incomplete data. Find them, listen to them and begin mapping a "happy path" to create an anchor in the process. Next, automate the happy path in RPA. Work to get that branch of the process working well and kick out any transaction that does not meet the happy path's strict criteria. We call these non-happy path situations "exceptions". After you are confident that the happy path is working well, give each exception type you identify a name and measure the volume of transactions that meet the key identifiers for that particular exception. Last, focus your attention on defining resolution steps for and automating the high-volume exceptions. As you can see, the process to tackle apparently complex processes is straightforward however, don't underestimate the level of effort required to define the initial happy path. RPA ultimately helps you turn unstable processes into clearly defined branches that can be understood and individually assessed for automation.

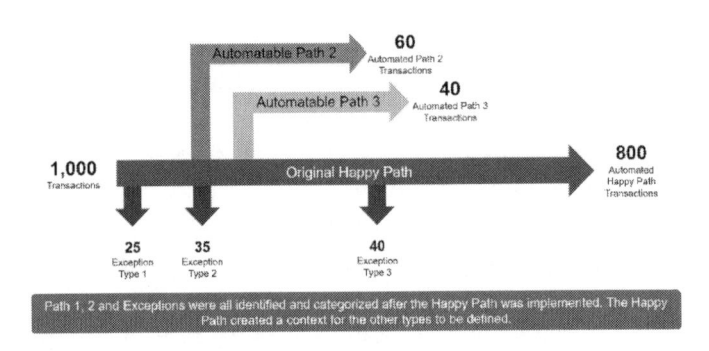

Figure 6.1 Happy Path Volume Mapping

Additional Criteria for RPA Candidate Selection and Prioritization

Basic RPA selection criteria can help you identify RPA opportunities quickly but there are other questions that can help you avoid investing a

Identifying RPA Opportunities | 39

lot of time and effort on the wrong process. The questions below are not always useful or necessary but they are good filters to leverage at your discretion.

Is there an upstream solution that could resolve the issue permanently?

Don't waste time on processes that have permanent solutions that can be built into core systems quickly and with low cost. If a permanent fix is a year or more a way and you can achieve value in the time remaining after an RPA solution is in place, it still may be worth the investment. Be cautious using RPA in these situations since the value you generate with RPA may make it harder to justify the cost associated with a permanent fix later.

Are there compliance challenges associated with the process?

Many times, compliance issues that persist within processes are costly to fix and have little to no return, but RPA may be able to lower the cost to implement a fix. The solution you create may be used later to prototype a more permanent solution in your core systems. By taking on the burden of figuring out the procedures to fix the compliance issue through RPA, you may lower the cost and effort required to implement a permanent solution.

Are there significant backlogs in the process?

Process backlogs represent the failure of the manual process to keep up with demand and indicates that there is some one-time value that may be achieved by implementing automation. If the backlogs are big enough, the one-time automation of backlog items may justify the cost to build an RPA solution in itself.

Does the process have data integrity issues?

Be careful with these types of processes. If the data integrity issues are being caused by human error as individuals try to consistently transform data, the process may be well suited for RPA. If the data integrity issues stem from a source of inconsistency like a poorly implemented OCR solution, the process may not be well suited for RPA. Make sure you understand why there are data integrity issues before working on these types of processes.

Is it a challenge to obtain operational data, metrics or key performance indicators (KPI) for this process?

Often times with complex manual processes, managers can't have their teams complete transactions and manually create categorization data or other metrics about each transaction at the same time. The choice boils down to whether or not the information gained from manually categorizing the transaction is worth the loss in overall productivity. Managers in these situations are under a lot of pressure to improve the average number of daily transactions each individual is able to complete and improve the accuracy of resolution. In processes with high fallout rates these pressures are amplified. Furthermore, the accuracy of manually entered categorization data may be suspect anyway if the rules about how to categorize each transaction are interpreted differently by each worker. The irony in these situations is that the only clear path to improving the processes is to create data about each transaction so the process can be well understood. Good managers will recognize this conflict but be unable to leverage their talents to solve the problem without the right tools. RPA can often help create the consistent metrics and categorization data needed to further improve the process. See the previous section discussing unstable processes.

Do other markets, countries or business areas operate similar processes?

Knowing just how prolific a particular process is across a company's business units can help prioritize a process more highly than it might have otherwise been. You may be able to pilot a solution for one market that can be deployed to others with some minor tweaks. Having a good idea about the reach of a process can help you multiply the value of your development effort and may shift your RPA program's overall priorities.

Does this process rely on OCR or non-form-based email?

You generally want to avoid using RPA in these situations. When it comes to OCR processes working in concert with RPA, the accuracy and consistency of the digitized outputs are extremely important. If you have doubts about the accuracy or consistency of the data that an OCR solution is creating, make these processes your last priority. Similarly, if the process requires analysis of unstructured emails to complete the transaction, send these to the bottom of your list as well. There are exceptions when it comes to unstructured, accurate, digitized text if you can leverage AI on the front end to impose an organization method on the unstructured data (post payment audit, for example) but don't expect RPA to be a good solution to these problems on its own.

Automated Opportunity Identification

Another alternative to the normal opportunity identification method is using tools that analyze the activities being performed on employee desktops. These tools are loaded on to desktops for a month or more to collect and categorize the flow of application interactions that employees use. The patterns that emerge can help you narrow down where people are swivel-chairing between applications and help identify places where automation would definitely make an impact. Tools like Skopiq will go a step further and help assign an estimated value to these interactions allowing you to quickly focus on the opportunities that will deliver real value. While this may sound like a silver bullet, the cost of using this approach could be comparable to engaging a consultant. Some RPA vendors will use these tools in the discovery phase at no charge to their potential clients. In either case, these techniques have the potential to be more accurate, targeted and effective than a traditional consulting engagement.

7

SELECTING A VENDOR

Selecting an RPA vendor can be a significant challenge for the uninitiated. There were advantages to delving into this space in 2015 because, at the time, adoption of RPA solutions was still in the fast-follower stage. There were less options and the frenzy to push the RPA easy button had not reached its peak. Today, there are significantly more RPA providers than in previous years and the peer pressure among senior leaders to adopt RPA has diminished the amount of deliberation they are willing to tolerate to get a program off the ground. These forces compel organizations down a well-worn, consultant dependent path that may be costly and unnecessary if you know how these consulting arrangements work and the characteristics of the vendor landscape as a whole. Let me give you an example.

Consultant Company X is a well-known and established international consulting firm however, few understand that their structure operates as a franchise model in practice. They have a central home office that provides support to their market leaders who lead consultant engagements for the region they are responsible for but may not have the expertise on their regional staff to address various knowledge gaps. These regional knowledge gaps are amplified with emerging technologies. This model presents many advantages since a long-term relationship can form between key leaders of companies within that region and Company X market leaders however, the structure of Company X creates incentives to engage you in a way that may not always be to your advantage.

In this situation Company X has a regional knowledge gap around RPA so when you come to them looking for advice on how to proceed with RPA, they will engage their home office experts. The home office experts will brief the regional leader on the topic and help them create a vision document and long-term engagement roadmap for your company. This roadmap will introduce the topic of RPA as a whole, discuss the value that can be created by RPA, amplify the challenges of deploying RPA and place an emphasis on how to become a world class implementer of this technology. The regional leader for Company X will deliver this sales pitch to your leaders arguing that you may be able to do this on your own but by working with Company X you can get to world class faster. Company X will then suggest that you engage their advisory services to help you build a custom roadmap of RPA initiatives and then reconvene to determine next steps.

Let's assume that you agree to allow them to help you build a roadmap for RPA. This initial engagement will probably take about 6 weeks and likely cost you between $80K to $150K. At the end of this engagement they will reconvene, emphasize the lack of talent and experience that your team has to get to world class on your own, unveil an RPA roadmap and suggest that the next step be to help you select a vendor. A discerning leader will ask what partnerships Company X has already formed with RPA vendors. Company X will likely reply that they have a preferred vendor, but they are confident that regardless of the vendor you choose, they will be able to support you. Many companies will take a step back from the consultant to evaluate the vendors for themselves and make a selection. For those that do engage Company X to help select an RPA vendor your looking at another 6 to 8-week engagement that will cost you another $80K to $150K.

If you're keeping track, you've spent between $160K and $300K and still have not created any value with RPA. Once a vendor is selected, Company X will offer to build out the most common and valuable RPA initiatives for you. At this point, they have evaluated and analyzed the potential value of each of the initiatives on your roadmap as part of their previous engagements. They know more about the value they should be able to achieve with each initiative better than you do. This is important to you because the price they quote you to build your RPA roadmap or outsource to them altogether is not one that analyzes their costs and then upcharges from there. Instead, they will often quote you a percentage of the anticipated savings which could be in the millions of dollars especially in the financial services space. Throughout the process, the regional leader is taking home a percentage of the fees collected from your engagements while the home office is generating revenue through the engagement of their subject matter experts.

This is a well-worn path that often results in a successful deployment of RPA, but it comes at a significant cost. The financial cost of trying to work through these problems yourself rather than engage a consultant to accelerate the process is the cost of engaging Company X minus the savings that might start to be generated faster than an in-house approach. From this perspective, you could hire one or two fulltime resources for a year to focus entirely on RPA for the cost of 12 weeks of consulting time. If you have a talented individual on your team you can tap to work on RPA on the side, the additional cost is to you is $0. Even if it takes your team longer to develop a roadmap and select a vendor, you gain dedicated institutional expertise that can be leveraged to accelerate your program into the future. You also build faith with your organization by entrusting them to take ownership of these new tools and methods.

The bottom line here is to think long and hard before using consulting firms as your "easy" button to advance an RPA program. The price you pay will reflect your lack of trust in your team and your ignorance of the topic. While this guide cannot help you with the first problem, use the information that follows as a way to push back against the potential costs of ignorance.

RPA Provider Types

Before creating your RFP and choosing which RPA providers you will engage, it is important to realize there are three main categories of RPA providers. There are niche providers, Business Process Outsourcers (BPOs) and Partnerships. Niche providers are companies that sell direct purchases of RPA software. Their value models vary as do their technical approaches to RPA, but they act and operate the same way you would expect any software vendor to act and operate. BPOs are companies like Xerox, Cognizant or Accenture who specialize in selling you an alternative to doing specific types of work in-house. They take your processes as they are, onboard them into their organization and drive value by making incremental improvements to performance over time. Another type of RPA provider is partnerships. Partnerships operate similarly to BPOs, but they are consultants first. Examples include Deloitte, Ernst and Young (EY), Price-Waterhouse-Cooper (PWC), KPMG and the list goes on. These consulting firms form partnerships with niche RPA vendors, but their business objective is to sell consulting services on the front end and deliver your roadmap with one of their RPA partners on the back end. Understanding the geography of RPA vendors is important before you begin vendor selection because understanding this landscape can help you interpret and properly consider which RPA approach best meets your needs.

Where Can I Get A Trustworthy List of RPA Vendors To Consider?

There are two industry standard ways to develop a trustworthy RPA vendor list: a Forrester Wave document or a Gartner Magic Quadrant document. Both of these reports will set you back $2,000 - $2,500 each but there are a few things to keep in mind before going down this path. First, Forrester and Gartner define the RPA space very differently and neither one of them take a holistic view of the vendor landscape. Forrester's evaluation only considers partnerships while Gartner's evaluation primarily considers niche providers. Second, you should never have to pay for a Forrester or Gartner product when you are building a vendor list. Forrester's "Wave" and Gartner's "Magic Quadrant" charts are both publicly available in various forums. Each chart plots the vendors on a grid so purchasing the full report is not necessary to simply build the list. If you want the full document, ask one of the vendors on the list that you want to evaluate to provide you a copy. Most vendors volunteer this information anyway so there is no need to spend money on these documents.

Vendors who are highly rated in these documents tend to push the fact very hard, but you need to make sure you understand what the documents are evaluating. I'll give you an example. The company I worked for needed to purchase a CRM system, so I led the vendor evaluation process. A vendor who was not on our list initiated contact with us in an attempt to throw their hat in the ring. The company was very well known for telecommunications infrastructure, but they were not on our radar because they did not have a CRM product that we were aware of. We agreed to meet and one of the first slides they presented us was a Forrester or Gartner chart (I forget which one it was). We had used the Forrester and Gartner charts for the CRM space to build our initial list so when they presented us with a chart that included them, I looked harder. What they were presenting was a Forrester / Gartner chart for communications infrastructure not CRM. They were selling a new CRM solution that was in its early development using their high ratings in communication infrastructure to mask the fact that they did not have a fully baked software offering. We did not add them to our list.

The moral of this story is to recognize that Forrester and Gartner products are tools built by companies that are influenced by the willingness of other companies to participate in their research and their own preconceptions about the geography of the vendor landscape. The way these two factors shape the final products can sometimes be unpredictable and head scratching. One example of where Forrester and Gartner products have blind spots are niche providers who specialize in a particular industry or functional area. Two examples that come to mind are Redwood and Olive AI. Redwood specializes in helping companies automate the end to end financial close process using RPA tools and was only recently added to these lists. Olive AI is a slick RPA tool focused on providing RPA services to the healthcare industry but to date is not included in their evaluations. Both vendors are worthy contenders for their prospective industry niches, but they do not fit the general definition of the RPA space as defined by Forrester and Gartner. While the Forrester Wave and Gartner Magic Quadrant are a much better option than a random Google search, you have to be discerning about the list of vendors you are presented with and recognize when there are obvious gaps.

Choose a Vendor Type

Before you reach out to vendors and ask them for demos of their products, your goal should be to narrow down your list to five vendors. Begin by taking your list of vendors and categorizing each one by type (niche, BPO or partnership) and Forrester / Gartner score (if applicable). The next step is to define your needs.

Niche vendors, BPOs and partnerships help you solve the same problem in very different ways, so you need to decide at the outset which direction you want to pursue. When you interact with niche vendors, you are purchasing software, pure and simple. Some niche providers will sell you software that has to be loaded on your own hardware while others will try to sell you cloud based RPA software. For example, Blue Prism sells software that is loaded on your infrastructure while Automation Anywhere provides partial cloud-based services. Both are considered leaders in the niche space, but they approach the RPA market very differently. With Blue Prism, you will need to load a controller application on each virtual machine and a designer / orchestration application on your process architects' personal computers. With Automation Anywhere, you do not have to load software on your virtual machines because the processes are run within their cloud infrastructure. You still have to load a designer application on a local desktop but there is not a virtual machine component. Beyond the differences in cost structure, the choice to go with a niche provider boils down to how successful you believe your team can be running an RPA program and the accompanying infrastructure on your own. If you have a strong technical team, cheap infrastructure and individuals on your team who can help define the pipeline, going with a niche RPA vendor may be a good option.

BPOs are selling you outsourcing services. They want you to hand over the day to day operations of entire business processes as they currently are and pay them less than you would pay a full-time dedicated team. They leverage their expertise in particular processes, their scales of economy and internally developed process automation tools (including RPA) to create the efficiencies they require to make a profit. BPOs have been using RPA tools behind the scenes for many years before RPA became a buzzword in corporate circles. They were the first to employ and master RPA tools and now use RPA as a selling point to prospective clients. For example, two different BPOs reached out to our company to discuss their RPA offering so we met with them to hear their sales pitches. After hearing their proposals, it was clear that they were not really selling RPA tools but rather leveraging the fact that they use RPA tools to try to convince us to outsource our processes. The proposed cost model was a classic, per transaction based BPO arrangement and had no resemblance to a niche provider's software licensing approach. The point here is that if you're willing to outsource the processes that your trying to automate, a BPO is a good option regardless of the tools they employ to achieve efficiencies for you.

We've already taken time to dissect the partnership arrangement. Think of partnerships as a consulting first approach to the problem. The consulting firms will help you get an RPA solution up and running but will start with consulting services then help you deliver the initial set of processes and in some cases then offer to be an outsourcer. This approach has the potential to be the most expensive route but if you do not have faith that your team can build and manage an RPA tool from day one and you are not considering an outsourcing model, a partnership may be a good approach for you.

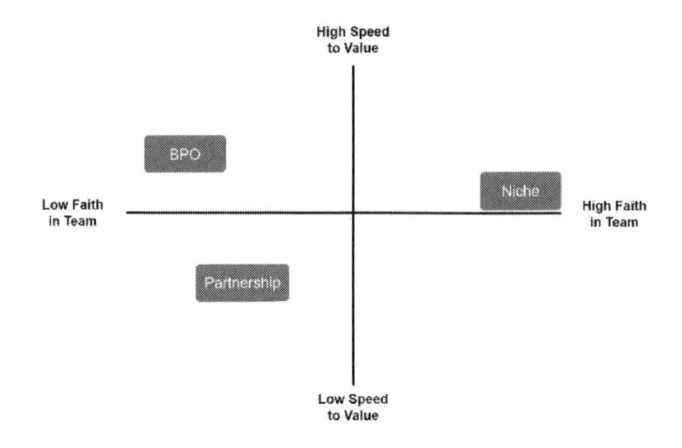

Figure 7.1 RPA Vendor Fit Grid

Why Evaluating 5 Vendors is Important

Once you've decided which RPA vendor type best matches your needs, you will want to choose 5 vendors that you want to get a more in-depth look at. There are several benefits to evaluating 5 different companies. First, you get a better sense for the proficiency of each company's sales team and technical team. There are many times when a vendor looks compelling on their website but when you meet the individuals selling, developing and delivering the product, it becomes very clear that they may not be a good fit. For example, some of the worst sales pitches and demos I've ever seen were delivered by vendors with whom we already had business and were exploring expanding our business with. These companies came off as entitled, unprepared and shocked when we began asking them detailed questions that they were unprepared to answer. Situations like this are red flags and interacting with more than one vendor helps you establish a baseline for which companies have it together versus others who may be bluffing.

The second reason evaluating 5 vendors is important is that it builds your expertise in the different variations of functionality that exist within this technical space. Assuming you have done your homework about RPA before you bring in vendors for demos, nothing can fully prepare you for the nuances that exist in the way each company operationalizes their tool. Some have better user interfaces for designing processes. Others have better orchestration modules and others have better scalability. You won't know 100% which vendor meets your expectations without hearing multiple sales pitches and seeing multiple demos.

The third reason you want to evaluate five vendors is that it gives you an opportunity to understand the different cost models that exist in this space. While a mature sales team will not give you a quote at this stage in the process, they should be willing to explain their billing and support model to you without discussing numbers. This information can be extremely valuable as you further narrow the field.

RPA Cost Models

There are three main cost models for RPA providers: per license, per transaction and per process. An emerging, less common cost model is an estimated percentage of value model leveraged by RPA-SAAS companies. The per license approach is common to niche vendors who sell software that gets loaded onto your VMs and local desktops. Often times there is a minimum threshold for the number of licenses you will have to purchase from these RPA providers and a minimum number of licenses to scale as well. What does this mean? RPA vendors who use this approach may say that you need to purchase a minimum of 10 licenses for your VMs and 1 to 2 licenses of the designer and orchestration program. They will often also set a minimum number of licenses that you must purchase once you need more than 10. The impact to you in this model is that you may be forced to purchase more RPA capacity than you are ready to tap from the outset and when you do get to the point where you are fully utilizing your initial purchase, you'll have to shell out again for even more excess capacity. There is a lot of waste in this model which makes having a roadmap defined very important.

Cost Models

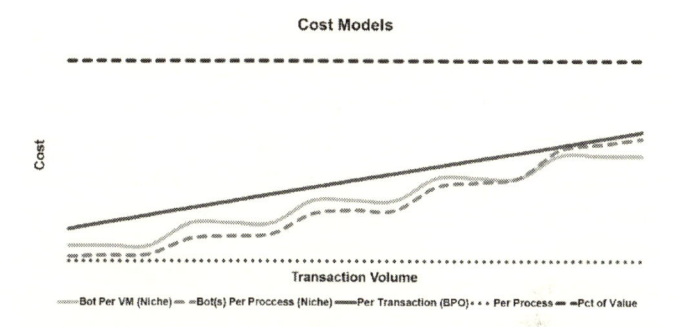

(chart showing cost vs. transaction volume with lines for: Bot Per VM (Niche), Bot(s) Per Proccess (Niche), Per Transaction (BPO), Per Process, Pct of Value)

Figure 7.2 RPA Cost Models

Another common cost model is the per transaction model. If you encounter an RPA provider that is selling a per transaction model, you may be dealing with a BPO. The per transaction model is extremely scalable and advantageous in the sense that you only pay for what you use rather than the software infrastructure itself. The problem with this arrangement comes when you have high, variable volumes that make it difficult for you to predict cost. Furthermore, the total benefit returned to your company can be significantly lower in this model if you're not careful. For example, let's say that automating a particular process saves you $5 per transaction. A vendor may quote you $0.25 per transaction which may seem reasonable on the surface until you compare it to the alternative billing models. What we found was that this arrangement was only advantageous compared to alternative cost models if we lowered the per transaction rate down to less than $0.05. Be very careful with these arrangements and do the math to figure out the opportunity costs for each approach.

The last billing model is a per process model. This model has a couple of variations including a pure per process arrangement regardless of the process load on your VMs versus a bot equals process approach. The pure per process arrangement, while the least common, has the potential to be the most financially beneficial approach if you are able to hold your cards close to your vest. What I mean by this is that if you allow the vendor to scope your prospective processes prior to agreeing on billing terms, they will price your processes very differently than they otherwise would. For example, many vendors will ask you for volume and staffing data related to your prospective processes prior to quoting your billing arrangement. It's a mistake to give them this information because it gives away one of your primary sources of leverage. If you are the only party that knows what the current state process volumes, staffing, average time to complete a process, error rates and backlogs are, you force the vendor to provide you a billing model that is based on their costs, not yours. Going further with this example, imagine that you know that if you are able to automate 30% of a current manual process end to end you will be able to save or avoid $5M annually. How do you think this knowledge will affect the RPA vendor's billing terms? They may try to charge you a percentage of the savings or quote you a per process amount that is significantly higher than they otherwise would have. Keeping tight control of this information means the only data they can orient pricing around are their hunches from past engagements and their own costs. Either way, it pays to keep this information closely guarded until the contract is signed.

Another dimension to keep in mind with pure per process arrangements is that you will have to work to develop a scale-based cost structure. Not every process represents the same amount of work. Some have higher volumes or complexity than others. Be prepared to negotiate pricing based on extra-large, large, medium and small processes usually with volume or processing time thresholds.

The variation to a pure per process billing model is a bot equals process billing model. This is the approach used by Automation Anywhere, one of the predominant RPA vendors today. The way it works is that each process you build is assigned a "bot" or multiple "bots" depending on the volume. Each bot can only run one process regardless of the size. The negative implication of this model is that you are essentially purchasing a partial VM from the vendor. What this means is that if you went with a niche RPA provider that loads software on your own VMs, you would be able to assign different processes to that VM on the fly as capacity becomes available. The benefit to the bot equals process approach is that the per bot cost is lower than a niche provider because of the fact that you can't leverage the excess capacity of the VM to do other processes. The decision you need to make revolves around how much work do you think you can manage through your own VM infrastructure. Once you have each vendor's billing model, you should be able to evaluate the opportunity costs and thresholds beyond which this model is no longer beneficial.

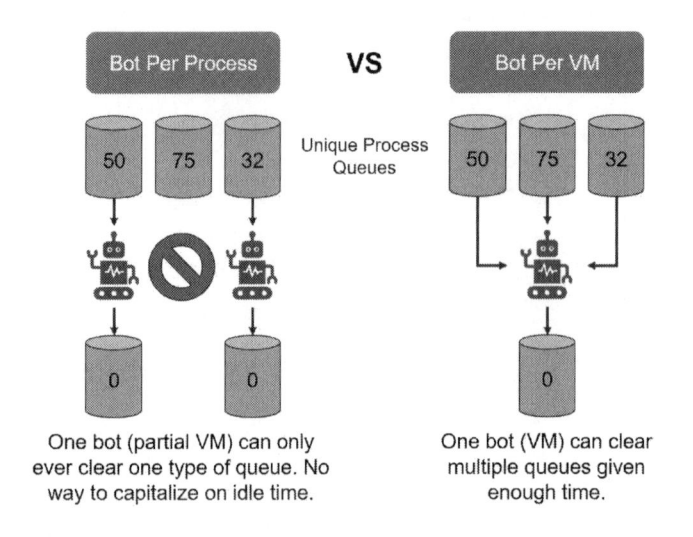

Figure 7.3 Bot Per Process vs. Bot Per VM

How to Evaluate Your Top 5 Vendors

Once you have narrowed down your list to 5 top RPA providers you will want to build a decision matrix, a post-demo survey and a user story guide. You will only use the decision matrix and post demo-survey for the second round but having the user story guide from the outset is helpful to help the less involved members of your team who are evaluating the vendor get some context for where the use of RPA is headed.

The decision matrix should be completed by no less than 5 key members of your team who are deeply engaged with the details of the vendor selection process. The goal of the decision matrix is to create an objective measure of the vendor's capabilities. While subjectivity can't be totally eliminated, the results of a decision matrix are much easier to justify with leadership and is better than going with your gut. When you build a decision matrix you will want to list out the key features and capabilities that are important to you. Major categories should include strategic investment, Forrester or Gartner scores, level of engagement, cost model, level of expertise required by the team, ease of use for process architects, ease of use of the orchestration module, type of data that can be secured within the tool and reporting capability. You will want to further stratify these categories to focus on the items that are most important to you. Once you have stratified these categories, you will need to assign weights to each category and subcategory. The max score should never go above 100.

Next you will need to build a post-demo survey. The purpose of this survey is to capture the general impressions of the tool. Everyone who participates in the vendor demo needs to complete the survey regardless of level of engagement in the overall process. The survey is the cost of admission into the demo because the feedback helps quantify the feeling people have about the vendor and the tool itself. The major questions in the survey that need to be asked are:

- Do you believe the vendor will be a good partner?

- Do you believe that the tool will meet our

needs?
- How difficult do you believe this tool would be to build and maintain?
- Would you recommend that leadership invest in this tool?

You should ask these questions on a numeric scale and then leave a comments section at the end to capture other thoughts and ideas.

How to Evaluate Your Top 3 Vendors

Your top 5 should be narrowed down to 3 remaining vendors. You may choose not to use the decision matrix to narrow the field from 5 to 3 but you should use the survey at a minimum. For the final three you will use the decision matrix and a user story guide to evaluate each vendor with the goal being to use this demo to narrow down the final two.

A user story guide is a document that outlines the various scenarios that you anticipate using an RPA tool for in a narrative format. Each use case should have details about each scenario along with some specific bullet points explaining features that you want to see in a follow up demo. Once complete, provide a copy of your guide to each vendor and ask them to come prepared to demonstrate these scenarios. Taking this approach is useful in a couple of ways. By giving each vendor the same scenarios, you know that they are all starting from the same place. This second demo becomes a reflection of the sales team's integration with their technical team and the level of agility their team has to meet demands that may change throughout the lifecycle of the partnership. Furthermore, a demo driven by your use cases goes beyond a sales pitch and helps you and your team visualize how a specific tool will operate in your environment.

After each vendor has given their user guide demo, complete a decision matrix on each one, send out the survey and eliminate the weakest vendor from consideration. You should be left with two top candidates that look strong and appear ready to meet your specific needs. The next step in the selection process is to run a proof of concept.

How to Evaluate Your Top 2 Vendors

At this stage in the selection process, you should feel very confident of the capabilities that exist in the broader market as well as the specific capabilities of your top vendors. However, running parallel proof of concepts is a great way to determine which tool will fit better in your environment before making a long-term commitment with an RPA provider.

The first thing you need for a proof of concept is a relatively simple process that will adequately prove the capabilities of each tool. Both vendors should work on the same process, have the same documentation provided to them and be given the same access to required resources. The key is not to give either vendor more information than the other about the process. Next, set a timeframe to complete the proof of concept. It is ideal if you can coordinate with both vendors at the same time, so you get a sense in the moment about how well each team is performing. The key metrics that you will want to measure are ease of implementation, speed of delivery, quality of outcome and FTE to bot efficiency ratios. FTE to bot efficiencies are measured on a per transaction completion time basis. You can expect a bot to be at least 3 times more efficient than a person because the bot can run 24/7. Your performance measure should compare how much greater than the baseline efficiencies you were able to achieve. It is not uncommon to see bots achieve 10 times the efficiency of an FTE.

While the proof of concept is progressing, request pricing quotes from each RPA vendor. You want to know the detailed charges prior to selecting a final vendor. The request is appropriate at this stage in the process and gives you leverage over both parties. They should never know the other vendor's quote so you should be in a strong position to negotiate to a cost structure that you believe is fair and sustainable. Remember, do not share any data about your process's volumes, FTE assigned to your processes or average FTE costs with your vendors. If you do, their quotes will be based on your costs, not theirs. They may have experience in your functional area and may have a rough idea of the value RPA can help you achieve but don't make it easy for them to leverage your data against you.

Selecting Your Top Vendor

At this point in the process you've amassed a lot of data about RPA vendors in general but have gleaned critical details about your top 2 candidates through a proof of concept. You should feel very confident about which vendor is right for you but before you pull the trigger there are a few more variables that you need to ensure are locked down and fully represented in your business case. This is the stage in the process where if you fail to communicate your findings in a way that decision makers in your organization can understand and feel comfortable advocating for through a budget request, much of your work may be fruitless.

While there is never a silver bullet for guaranteeing your request for RPA investment will be successful, you can maximize your chances by having clear decision matrix results, representing the impressions of the broader team through a survey, communicating the results of your proof of concept with metrics and building a holistic three year value model. Decision matrix results draw out the opinions of your technical teams in a way that is easy for your leaders to understand. The survey results represent what the broader team felt about the tool. Communicating the efficiencies achieved by each vendor as well as the hands-on experience deploying the tool during the POC helps leaders visualize how the RPA tool you're recommending will be operationalized in your environment. All of these elements are important but if you cannot represent your recommendation in financial terms, this work may not matter in the end.

8

BUILDING YOUR BUSINESS CASE

Building a business case for this type of initiative is all about creating contrast with alternative investments. Your leaders may not have the budgets to make an investment in RPA without your finance organization giving the green light. Furthermore, if you have not properly engaged your IT organization up to this point, you may find yourself at square one if they decide that your work did not consider broader enterprise concerns. The goal when you are building a value model or business case is to arm your leaders with the information they need to advocate for investment.

The place to start is by having a discussion with

your finance and Portfolio Management Office (PMO). Finance will be able to tell you if you need to work with someone on their team to build the business case and who that person is. It's better to have this conversation up front rather than go off and spend a lot of time and effort building a business case that does not meet their standards. You should also engage your PMO team if you will need PM resources to understand how these requests normally progress through prioritization. There are situations where leaders may grab on to your idea and champion it outside of the normal red tape but, especially if your leaders are less technically proficient and do not immediately grasp the value of RPA, working with the right teams from the beginning can help win them over.

So, let's say that your finance team gives you the green light to build a draft business case (they may also call it a proforma). The first thing you want to do is lay out your current and anticipated future costs. The main categories of cost you want to include are people costs, operating expenses and capital expenses. People costs should include the current FTE performing work that you believe can be automated times the average rate of pay for those FTE. You will also need to estimate the future FTE required after automation times the average rate of pay. Next you should list all of the operating expenses associated with the current FTE usually expressed as a percentage of per capita FTE cost. This covers current run-the-business expenses like communications infrastructure, IT equipment, software and printing material. Once you've defined current opex for effected FTE, define the same numbers for the future state. Next, list the one-time capital expenditures that you may need along with any one-time project team costs and ramp costs to get the new operating model working.

After defining these costs, contrast the current state costs against the future state costs to develop your anticipated cost avoidance value. If the process you are automating generates income somehow, as may be the case in a post-payment-audit scenario, be sure to include the current income created subtracted from future anticipated income to define income-based value as well. Next build your costs and value estimates into a cashflow model that can then be further expressed in terms of Net Present Value and Internal Rate of Return. Your final step should be to review and refine this model with your finance team prior to presenting the business case and results of your POC to your leadership.

While the process of building a business case is not too difficult, the implications of how RPA generates value are controversial and not to be underestimated or minimized. Make no mistake about it. RPA primarily creates value by automating work that current employees perform. Much of the RPA literature out there including academic literature seeks to play down the negative impacts that any one RPA initiative may have while at the same time making broad statements about the impact to the workforce in the next 10 years. Playing down the impact of individual initiatives while sounding a warning about the overall impact of automation on the global workforce is duplicitous. Let me repeat and be absolutely clear. RPA primarily generates value by automating tasks performed by current employees.

With that said, a discerning leader can acknowledge the fact that RPA primarily generates value by impacting work that employees perform and largely avoid the negative consequences of this reality. There are a few ways to do this. First, try to capture the value of RPA in terms of avoiding future hires. In this case, the value generated is real albeit slower to mature and can be measured but the impact to current employees is eliminated. Second, if avoiding future hires is not possible, having a specific plan to transition impacted staff to other priorities within your organization or your company more broadly can avoid many of the negative ramifications of automation. While restructuring can be tricky, many of the employees who engage in work that RPA is automating are problem solvers, can acquire new knowledge quickly and are already familiar with your company. Last, there are many instances where what is being automated through RPA is net new work that has never been performed by employees or has been inconsistently performed because of the volume or difficulty of that particular task. In these instances, there is no impact on your current workforce but there is avoided cost. In restructure and cost avoidance scenarios, finance may be the biggest obstacle to following through since they want to express savings in terms of return on invested capital. However, I have found that top level leaders in these situations are very keen on avoiding negative impacts to their current workforce and will usually work through these situations with a great deal of sensitivity. Letting a large swath of your team go is not a feather in the cap that most leaders want.

One of the common ways that leaders mitigate the labor impacts of RPA is by reallocating the savings to other, more strategic roles. Keep in mind that the new roles often require higher wages than the roles reduced by RPA. In these situations the organization can easily end up spending more on labor than they spent prior building an RPA workflow. If finance chooses to link the RPA savings and the subsequent reallocation of labor, the net savings may not be anywhere near expectations. While this does not happen in every instance, staying connected to your finance partner is key to ensuring the savings you claim is validated and recognized.

9

DEPLOYING RPA

After you have selected an RPA tool you will need to build your team, build your intake process and deliver your roadmap. If you have chosen to acquire a niche tool as opposed to outsource or work through a partner, the strength of the team you build will ultimately determine the success of your RPA program. The key roles that you need to fill are Process Designers, Process Builders and Data Analysts. This is not to say each of these roles needs to reside on a centralized team, but you need resources who fulfill each function.

Building Your Team

Process Designers are individuals who build the process flows that will ultimately be translated into an automation. The difficulty with these process flows as opposed to process flows that are more familiar are that the Process Designer will need to document down to the keystroke level detail. This role requires individuals who may not have much programming background or skill but appreciate machine logic and the attention to detail required to translate a manual process into an automated product. Individuals with process improvement backgrounds fit this mold well. The one caveat to watch out for with those who have Lean or Six-Sigma backgrounds is that creating a perfect process map before you build the automation may actually slow down your ability to deliver value. Individual with process improvement backgrounds will tend to attempt to map all possible branches of the process rather than defining a happy path, deploying it then iterating through the other branches. It's important to help these individuals adapt to the idea that automating a part of the process flow can actually help you understand the other branches faster.

Process Designers are typically found either in the functional area that you are building automations for or IT Solutions Architects. Either one can work but because of the nature of the work being automated, there are more long-term advantages to the organization as a whole if the Process Designers are members of the business rather than IT. The business is automating a process at the keystroke level detail which means that you want people within the business line who intimately understand how the automation was built. Unlike designing integrations between two systems where IT expertise is absolutely necessary, the steps RPA automates are core business activities that the business should understand firsthand. Another advantage to having Process Designers from the business side is that if you ever decide to build the automation into your ERP system or another more permanent mechanism, you have a resource on the team who can give clear requirements to your IT partners. IT Solutions architects can absolutely do this work and do it well. However, there are some advantages to this role being filled by talented individuals from within the business line itself.

While the level of expertise required for your Process Builder varies somewhat depending on which tool you select, many vendors recommend that you fill these roles with people who build macros, SQL or Python scripts. The reason you want people like this to build your RPA solutions is that they are likely already invested in many of the problems that are on your RPA roadmap, have demonstrated a knack for finding a way to automate process segments and are often intrinsically motivated. The presence of scripting is often an indicator of where RPA can add value. It means that the business has naturally developed a survival mechanism to combat the lowest hanging transactional work. Often times, there is a strong desire to automate more of the process but the progress stalls because of the limitations of whatever scripting tool is being leveraged. Common challenges with scripting languages include the limited ability to string an end to end process across multiple applications, the inability to create dynamic data triggers to initiate the script, the lack of a scheduling mechanism, spotty reporting and a lack of audit accountability. Individuals who are contributing to your company by scripting through these challenges will be eager to use a tool with capabilities that match their ambitions and come with insider knowledge about many of the initiatives on your RPA roadmap. These individuals are usually intrinsically motivated because they have had to fight for time to build these scripts in between day to day tasks. People on your team who use scripting tools to automate pieces of your processes today are ideal for Process Builder roles.

Last but not least, you will need Data Analysts to help you fully leverage and represent the massive amount of information your RPA processes will produce. These individuals will ensure that the way your data is being represented adds value to leaders who will make decisions based on this data. Many times, the Data Analyst also supports the Process Builder with the orchestration aspects of the RPA process by helping set up or maintain the scheduling and load balancing functions. These are natural tasks for the Data Analyst because it is often their analysis that helps drive the optimization of bot load balancing and scheduling.

Once you are confident that you have the skills available to sustain an RPA function you will have to decide whether to centralize or confederate your RPA function. Your organization may make the decision to have all RPA development centralized across the enterprise or decide to allow RPA development within each functional area. Either approach can work but the problems you encounter managing the program will differ in each scenario. If your organization chooses a centralized model for the enterprise the challenge will be prioritizing very different requests from each functional area. The irony of a centralized model is that it can defeat one of the main purposes of RPA if the prioritization and delivery of automation initiatives does not help the functional areas that typically don't get prioritized for other automation work. RPA is intended to help your organization go after initiatives that will not create a return using other methods of automation. If the enterprise RPA team ends up focusing on functional areas that regularly get the time, attention and investment from other means of automation, there are opportunities that are being missed.

Another challenge with a centralized model is that many times, the use cases for RPA are finite. There are not an inexhaustible set of use cases for an RPA tool so the danger in creating a centralized team is that they may eventually run out of use cases that justify the value of that team. There will always be monitoring and controlling work that needs to be done through the orchestration module, but the development aspects of RPA may eventually drop off. That being said, most organizations probably have between 3 to 5 years' worth of RPA work minimum if they have not already begun the RPA journey but it is important to recognize from the outset that RPA work is not infinite.

On the other hand, your organization may agree

to allow RPA development to take place within each functional area. The immediate challenge of this model is governance. For functional teams to successfully deploy RPA solutions requires leadership from IT to outline the minimum requirements that each organization must adhere to. In this model, IT needs to lay the ground rules for security, compliance, audit, testing and the approval process for moving an automation that interacts with core systems into production. Establishing governance for RPA in a decentralized model takes time and persistence especially when your IT organization is unfamiliar with RPA. However, the effort is worth the reward if in the end your company is able to move faster to deploy RPA automations of various levels of value versus waiting in a queue to get prioritized like any other automation request.

The confederated model at the enterprise level also forces functional areas to wrestle with the extent to which their RPA development teams will be centralized. In these situations, there is a level of central management required to implement RPA effectively especially if RPA is being deployed in multiple countries or markets. Often times each country or market will require different considerations for the same processes because of local legal constraints. In these scenarios, a relatively small central team will need to help manage the efforts of distributed local teams. The difficulty in this model is how to determine which roles to centralize. At a minimum, the centralized RPA team should maintain some level of audit oversight and have the final say with IT to move automations into production.

Ultimately, building and sustaining your RPA team can be the most challenging aspect of getting an RPA program off the ground. Finding the right mix of talent, deciding the degree to which you will centralize the RPA function and deciding how you manage demand across geographies are complex questions to answer. However, with persistence and the right people at the table, you can form a team that meets the demands of your organization and delivers value consistently.

Building Your Intake Process

RPA intake processes are similar to almost any project intake process you may have experienced. First, you will want to use a set of pre-determined criteria to pre-screen the requests that you are getting from your organization. As mentioned earlier, there are a clear set of questions to consider when evaluating each request and how well they match with RPA. Second, building out an ROI model for each initiative that meets the RPA criteria will be an important input to determining priority in your backlog. Next, you may have resources that you can leverage to begin documenting the process at key stroke level detail so that your Process Builders can hit the ground running once they are available. Ideally all of these steps will be managed inside a tool that helps you track both the request and the progress being made toward delivering the request. Again, the RPA intake process is not rocket-science and follows the established patterns for other intake processes.

Deliver Your Roadmap

Delivering your roadmap begins with picking a couple of quick wins to convince those in your organization who were not a part of the proof concept or the selection process that RPA can produce value. While this may lead you to pick a couple of initiatives that do not prioritize as well against others, it's important to establish the credibility of the program with your broader organization and your newly formed team. Few things solidify the interest, energy and loyalty of an organization to a program like quick, tangible examples of delivered value. It also helps galvanize your team and set a marker down for expectations of quality and speed to market. Eventually, once you know your team's capacity to deliver, you may want to implement a release cycle but use the early initiatives to develop an estimated rate of delivery that can help you determine what release schedule will work best for you. The last principle to keep in mind is to always remember that RPA is process-automation duct tape. While some organizations may regard it as a permanent fixture, moving your RPA solutions into an ERP system or other core system is a more permanent automation method. The value is not always there to transition an RPA solution into a core system but consider RPA as a core systems prototyping solution wherever practical.

10

SMALL BUSINESSES AND RPA

One of the large, untapped markets for RPA is small businesses. Where else can you find a larger hodge-podge of disparate systems that don't share information well all being held together by human effort? Add to this the fact that many of these mundane tasks are not ones that add bottom line value to the business owner but still must be done, you have a large, motivated market ripe for automation.

There are several challenges to overcome to apply RPA to small businesses. First, while the market is large, the needs are not uniform from business to business. Companies attempting to build automations for small businesses may not find a lot of synergies from one client to the next. Second, to bring down the marginal costs of the software and infrastructure for small business owners would require specialized companies to negotiate Services Provider License Agreements (SPLAs) with each RPA vendor that they use. This is a significant barrier to entry because of the sweat equity involved on the front end to get this off the ground. Third, the support model for central delivery of custom RPA solutions for small business would be difficult to overcome.

All of the negatives aside, I'm still surprised that there are not more vendors looking to tap into this potential market. I've only been able to find one (qBotica out of Phoenix Arizona) so far in my research and would hope that there are more on the horizon. Unlike automation innovations in the past, RPA has the potential to empower main street businesses rather than pillage them. We'll see if it lives up to the potential.

11

HISTORICAL AND ETHICAL CONSIDERATIONS

RPA does not exist within an ethical or historical vacuum. The need for RPA arises from legitimate business demands but brings with it a wave of implications about the ethical use and historical significance of this toolset. It is very important to consider the implications of RPA in both a historical and ethical context because to do anything less is irresponsible especially for senior leaders in corporate environments. To date, I have been encouraged by the degree of sensitivity senior corporate leaders I have worked with while deploying RPA have demonstrated. The weight of interest and sensitivity must continue to exist as a balance against a reckless pursuit of value without regard to the long-term ramifications for loyal employees.

What Is The 4th Industrial Revolution and Why Does It Matter?

The 4th Industrial Revolution is best explained by Klaus Schwab who is one of the originators of the term and the head of the World Economic Forum. In his book, "The Fourth Industrial Revolution", Dr. Schwab explains that the first industrial revolution transformed the way tasks typically performed using muscle power (people or animals) got accomplished. Muscle power was converted to mechanical power. The second industrial revolution transformed the way we organized mechanical energy through the invention of the assembly line. The third industrial revolution introduced digital computing and information storage to the world. Last but not least, the 4th industrial revolution leverages data and connected digital devices to broaden the reach of automation into activities that have not been accessible to this point in history.

Historical and Ethical Considerations | 83

	First	Second	Third	Fourth
Years	1760 - 1840	Late 1800s – Early 1900s	1960 – 1990's	2000's - Present
Key Features	Mechanical Muscle	Mass Production	Digital Computing and Info Storage	IoT, Data Leverage, Application Diversity
Examples	Trains, Steam Engine	Cars, Assembly Lines	Mainframes, PCs, Processors, Databases	Connected Devices, AI, Apps

Figure 11.1 Industrial Revolution Grid

There is an observable pattern that emerges from each revolution. Physical technology evolves to create new tools (First, Third) that are then optimized by leveraging information (Second, Fourth). We are in the midst of an explosion of innovation around how to more efficiently leverage the computing power and data storage capacity pioneered between the 1960's through the 1990's. In many ways the rise of centralized data/computing centers that enable the internet and software as a service (SAAS) acted as a primary transitional technology that enabled the explosion of application development we see today. This boom is the modern equivalent of the emergence of mass production from the mechanical innovations that preceded it. New tools emerge that then need time to become ubiquitous and cheap which ushers in mass movements of innovation which optimize the application of those tools. Understanding this pattern helps contextualize the emergence of quantum computing which in itself could represent the cornerstone of what may become the 5th industrial revolution.

Regardless of future developments, the current software application boom is the primary condition that made the emergence of RPA tools inevitable since RPA helps solve for the urgent need to bridge gaps between applications. Business processes create the context through which these applications can be unified to create transactional outcomes. Up until now, people or costly, custom data integrations have filled the role of software mediators. Unfortunately, in many business contexts, people are not well suited to perform these tasks consistently, quickly or accurately.

In short, the 4th Industrial revolution matters because it represents a boom in the optimization of how we fully leverage the potential of information computing and storage infrastructure. As technology developers push the limits of what current tools can do, there are significant tradeoffs between the human skills required to successfully navigate a sub-optimized technology environment and companies that adopt the rapidly expanding means of information leverage. For many, the journey between the skill demands of yesterday and the new demands of the present will not be an easy path. The difficulties of re-skilling are amplified by the broad impact emerging tools have on high-paying, white collar, middle-class jobs. Without a clear understanding of the implications of these dynamics on people, the ethical principles required to transform how business is done while giving due consideration to the individuals impacted by transformation will remain elusive.

The Challenge of Re-skilling a Workforce

Historical and Ethical Considerations | 85

The need to transform skillsets to optimize the interactions between people and machines is not new. Each industrial revolution has redefined the set of high demand skills required to maximize value and each revolution has put unique pressures on individuals with depreciating skillsets. While the shift in demands for what skills companies are willing to pay high wages for does not happen overnight, workers with depreciating skillsets are uniquely challenged to understand the dynamics that are reshaping the conditions of their work, reframe the relevance of their skills, grapple with loss of identity and decide how best to meet these challenges.

Skillset demands do not transform instantly but the pace of change is accelerating. The first two industrial revolutions lasted approximately 30 years and where followed by a 50-year period of consolidation. The 3rd industrial revolution lasted about 30 years as well but immediately transitioned into the 4th industrial revolution. While it remains to be seen whether the consolidation period between industrial revolutions is gone forever it is important to recognize that our economy has been fundamentally transforming its skill demands for the last 50 years with no end in sight. The demand for new skills is not new, is always happening and though accelerating is a process that takes many years to affect the economy in aggregate.

I believe the primary reasons that transforming high demand skills takes time are the knowledge gaps of senior leaders, industry trends and the emergence of new centers of gravity. Senior leaders will typically be very adept at navigating the challenges of past economic paradigms. This means that existing companies can only transform as quickly as senior leaders adapt to the new paradigms. The process of educating key leaders about how to respond to the forces of change is a process that inherently takes time and varies by industry. Each industry has different anchors in the current economic paradigm, and some are easier to shift than others. Industries that generate value through information have less holding them to the current paradigms than industries with large physical capital requirements. Beyond senior leaders and industry trends, each industrial revolution requires companies to emerge that force the acceleration of change. These centers of gravity pull otherwise reluctant industries into the new paradigm by directly competing with them or by attracting talent away from lagging industries.

Individuals with depreciating skillsets may be lulled into a false sense of security because of the time it takes for new skill demands to become ubiquitous or, worse yet, not even realize that changes are underway. As such, the initial challenge for workers with depreciating skillsets is to become aware of the changing skills landscape and accurately assess how these changes may impact them. The danger here is that workers may not have a reason to ask tough questions about the durability of their current skills until it is too late. All too often, the moment individuals realize the value of their skills is not a good match for the changing economic environment is the moment their position is impacted in some way.

Having a position eliminated or being let go takes an emotional toll on workers with depreciating skillsets that may impact their ability to quickly adapt and move forward. One of the practical impacts of an identity crisis is that individuals don't accurately assess the true value of their skills to the market. Some will be in denial and will over value their skills compared to the market while others will allow pessimism to lead them to undervalue their skills. In either situation, there is an emotional toll to becoming a casualty of shifting skill demands.

The last challenge individuals with depreciating skillsets face is identifying the best strategy for adapting to market changes. Some will run to degree programs and certifications while others will seek to ride out the changes and hope they can survive long enough to retire. Acquiring new skill sets is not an easy proposition and can be full of peril since there is not a single path that will guarantee a successful transition for every individual.

The challenges facing transitioning workforces are significant, perilous, slow but accelerating. The onus falls on corporate leaders to leverage their authority and influence to chart a path for all employees to be sustainably successful. There is no one size fits all solution but there are ethics-based principles that can help mitigate the consequences of automation for workers.

Ethical Principles for Mitigating Automation Consequences

Leaders of organizations implementing job impacting automation initiatives have a key role in mitigating as many of the negative consequences for their current employees as possible. Leaders are in a unique position to influence not just what gets automated but more importantly how ideas get automated. The effectiveness of these mitigation strategies depends on a leader's ability to influence the way automation value is assessed by finance, being consistently transparent about the forces shaping your business and developing a culture of continuous learning.

Proactively Frame the Value Context

The way finance defines the value of automation will set the context for any employee impacts that follow. If the business case is accepted on the basis of reducing FTE, employee reductions will be expected. If the business case is accepted on the basis of preventing projected FTE growth, employee reductions may not be a necessary outcome. The ability to tune the value proposal of RPA in a way that mitigates impact to employees requires a well-considered strategic plan and a willingness to work through the challenges that will inevitably come from finance. Without a strategic plan that defines where future FTE growth will occur it will be very difficult to convince finance to approve automation investment as a cost avoidance strategy.

Even if leaders have a clear strategy that outlines

anticipated FTE growth, they will have to take the time to work through the legitimate challenges that will come from finance since anticipated FTE growth cannot improve return on invested capital unless these projections are already built into the budget. Employee reductions are not a forgone conclusion to justify an investment in RPA however, without foresight and planning, time constrained automation investment proposals will gravitate naturally toward employee reductions as the means of capturing value. Leaders must work to proactively frame the value context by having strategic vision, fighting the urge to push the FTE reduction easy button and being willing to work with finance in order to prevent negative impacts to their current employees.

Educate Teams About the Forces Shaping Your Business

Leaders must take on the role of educators when it comes to helping the teams they oversee understand the forces that are shaping your business. Without an ongoing, transparent dialogue about the challenges and opportunities of automation, employees may not take the necessary steps to continuously develop new skillsets. There is a fine line between creating fear of job impacts and empowering your team with the knowledge they need to inspire continuous learning, but this is a challenge leaders must accept. Open conversations about the future of work and what it may look like for employees can create a context of collaboration around keeping skills current and relevant. If employees see keeping skills current as a shared responsibility between the company and the individual, the organization will be much better prepared to weather future automation impacts.

Another key to keeping open dialogue with employees is to avoid false narratives about automation "lifting the burden of repetitive tasks" from employees. Many employees love these repetitive tasks and would be happy to continue doing them if given the opportunity. It is more important for leaders to help their employees accept the reality of automation by calling on them to keep their skills current than to perpetuate weak justifications for automation.

Develop a Continuous Learning Culture

A continuous learning culture is about preparing every day for the inevitable shifts in employee skill demands. Rather than wait for automation or other initiatives to compel investments in reskilling employees, building a culture that expects employees to hone their skills consistently can prepare employees for the worst-case scenario. Consistent skill development also allows organizations to re-absorb employees impacted in one area of the business back into other areas of the business more easily. Continuous learning is not optional for leaders who want to safeguard their current employees against the economic forces reshaping the way they work.

12

CONCLUSION

RPA is a powerful and misunderstood tool that can bring many benefits to organizations trying to simplify the automation of workflows. RPA is not AI but will often be sold that way. RPA providers vary in their value proposition, methods of delivery and ability to meet the unique constraints of your business. Selecting a tool is only the beginning of the process of operationalizing RPA. To get the most out of RPA tools requires a deep understanding of your end to end processes and the value associated with various problems that RPA is well suited to solve. RPA cannot be implemented in a vacuum since it impacts the work people are accustomed to doing on a fundamental level. Real leadership is required to guide RPA to its full potential and mitigate the impacts to your existing workforce.

ABOUT THE AUTHOR

Jonathan Sireci, PMP, CSM is the founder of Farchair Solutions, a consulting firm that focuses on making tools and techniques commonly used in corporate settings accessible to small businesses. Jonathan is an Air Force Academy graduate who spent six and a half years as an active duty officer before transitioning into corporate back-office management roles leading large technology deployments in the retail and healthcare industries.

Made in the USA
Columbia, SC
14 January 2021